The Storming of Fort Wagner

BLACK VALOR IN THE CIVIL WAR

1652

The Storming of Fort Wagner

BLACK VALOR IN THE CIVIL WAR

IRVING WERSTEIN

FIREBIRD BOOKS

SCHOLASTIC BOOK SERVICES
A Division of Scholastic Magazines, Inc.

Library of Congress Catalog Card Number: 76-116626

Copyright © 1970 by Irving Werstein. All rights reserved. Published by Scholastic Book Services, a division of Scholastic Magazines, Inc.

1st printing .... July 1970

Printed in the U.S.A.

To Lizette and Leonard Safranek
with gratitude and love.
And to Steven for his faithfulness.

ACKNOWLEDGEMENTS

I wish to give thanks to the staffs of the New York Historical Society, the New York Public Library, and the Historical Division of the U.S. Army.

I also owe thanks to Lilian Moore and Barbara Walker, my editors; to my agent, Candida Donadio; to Henry Chafetz and Sidney B. Solomon; and to all the thoughtful and gracious people who were ready with suggestions and encouragement.

CONTENTS

1 Black Soldiers for the Union Army?

For two years the United States had been a nation divided, broken in two. Brother had turned against brother. Since 1861, North and South had been locked in a bloody Civil War.

"Two years!" people sighed.

They thought of all the places where young men's lives had been lost—Shiloh, Manassas, Antietam. Once those places had been just names to most Americans. Now the long list of men killed and wounded there had made them words of dread.

"When will the killing end?" asked fathers and mothers, wives and sweethearts. Sometimes they spoke the words aloud. Sometimes they said them hopelessly to themselves. The war seemed to have a life of its own. Once started, it went on and on.

At the beginning, in 1861, young men of the North and South had been eager to get into the fighting. Southerners had flocked to enlist in the Confederate Army, Northerners to join the Union Army. By the end of 1862 they were far less eager on both sides. Some knew that their brothers were now dead. Others had lost friends. The lists of dead and wounded grew longer and longer. The flood of volunteers slowed down to a trickle. In despair, the South was beginning to *draft* men into the Confederate Army.

The North was not ready to do the same. Not yet. President Abraham Lincoln was calling for 300,000 men to volunteer for the Union Army.

As time went on, it became clear that nowhere near 300,000 men would volunteer. The men were needed. Where were they to come from?

"Let the slaves and free colored people be called into service, and formed into a liberation army!" This is what Frederick Douglass urged as soon as the war began. Douglass, a great leader of his people, had escaped from slavery. He knew how his people felt. "We are ready," he said to the whites, "but you won't let us go."

It was true. Black men wanted to fight. As soon as the first shot had been fired, free black men of Boston had tried to enlist in the army. They were refused. In New York black men formed their own regiments and offered their services. They were turned down by the U.S. Army. In Pittsburgh, in Cleveland, in Providence, in Philadelphia, in Detroit, black men by the hundreds and thousands asked to

Confederate General Robert E. Lee, 1807-1870

Ulysses S. Grant, 1822-1885
U.S. General and 18th President

fight. They begged the government to take them. But President Lincoln's Secretary of War said, "This department has no intention to call into the service of the government any colored soldiers."

Lincoln knew that black men wanted to fight. He also knew *why* they wanted to fight. They wanted to help kill slavery. But the President was determined to keep the question of slavery out of the war. And to do that, he had to keep black men out of the war.

The President told the South the same thing that he told the North: we fight to "preserve the Union." What did he mean?

11

The southern states were gone. They had left the Union to set up their own government. Now, they were the Confederate States of America. The Union was split in two. Now, the United States was no safer than a table trying to stand on two legs. Lincoln would do anything to get the southern states back before the Union toppled.

The President also knew that most white people in the North did not want black men to be soldiers. One Union man with the 74th New York Volunteers wrote, "We don't want to fight side by side with them. We think we are a too superior race for that."

There was another reason the President wanted to keep quiet about slavery and black soldiers. He was thinking of the States on the border between the North and the South—the states that had not yet joined the South. In these states bordering on the North there were Unionists, people who were on the side of the North. But, at the same time, many of these Unionists were slave owners. The President didn't want to do anything that would turn these Unionists in the border states against him. He thought he needed their help to defeat the South.

So, for many reasons, President Lincoln kept refusing to let northern states form black regiments.

Nevertheless, in the North, black men—and women too—were already taking part in the war. They were not soldiers. They had no guns. Instead they worked behind the lines. They drove wagons delivering supplies, dug outdoor toilets, built forts and roads. Some were personal servants to officers. Others cooked and washed clothes.

In the South too black people helped in the war. The Confederate Army used both slaves and free blacks. It didn't matter that the law said a man was free. If he was black, he was forced to work for the Confederacy. Six Confederate states even passed laws forcing free black men to work for the army.

Black people were very important to the South. Slaves worked behind the army lines. They worked on the plantations. They grew food so the soldiers could eat. They grew cotton so the soldiers could have clothes. Because there were slaves to do this work, white men could be used to fight.

As a result, the South had so many white men fighting that the North wondered if the Confederates had a secret weapon! Indeed, the South did have a weapon—slaves. Thousands and thousands of strong black people working night and day.

In the South, black people were being forced to help the Confederacy. But, in the North, where three hundred thousand soldiers were needed, black men were asking to fight for the Union.

Recruit black troops? To army leaders in Washington this seemed unthinkable.

"But in the navy," one of the military men in Washington hesitantly brought out, "black men are doing *combat duty*."

A NATION DIVIDED—1860-1861

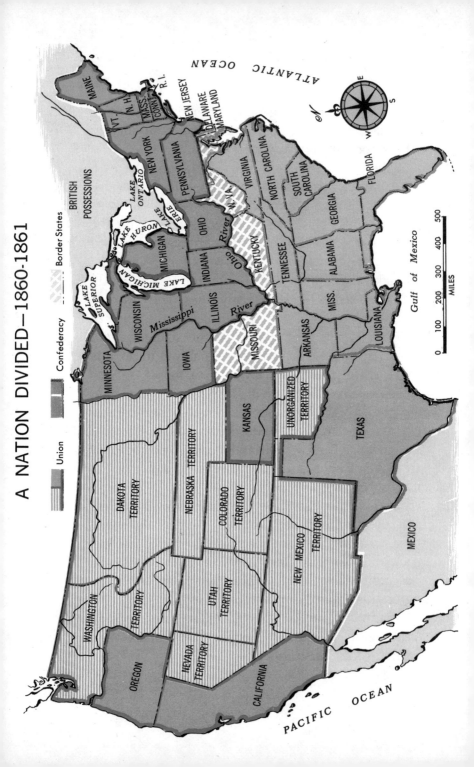

Union

Confederacy

Border States

N
E
S
W

ATLANTIC OCEAN

PACIFIC OCEAN

Gulf of Mexico

BRITISH POSSESSIONS

MEXICO

MAINE
VT.
N. H.
MASS.
CONN.
R. I.
NEW YORK
NEW JERSEY
PENNSYLVANIA
DELAWARE
MARYLAND
VIRGINIA
W. VA.
NORTH CAROLINA
SOUTH CAROLINA
GEORGIA
FLORIDA
ALABAMA
MISS.
TENNESSEE
KENTUCKY
OHIO
INDIANA
ILLINOIS
MICHIGAN
WISCONSIN
MINNESOTA
IOWA
MISSOURI
ARKANSAS
LOUISIANA
TEXAS
KANSAS
UNORGANIZED TERRITORY
NEBRASKA TERRITORY
DAKOTA TERRITORY
COLORADO TERRITORY
NEW MEXICO TERRITORY
UTAH TERRITORY
NEVADA TERRITORY
CALIFORNIA
OREGON
WASHINGTON TERRITORY

LAKE ONTARIO
LAKE ERIE
LAKE HURON
LAKE MICHIGAN
LAKE SUPERIOR

Ohio River
Mississippi River

MILES
0   100   200   300   400   500

That was a fact. From the beginning of the war, the U.S. Navy had encouraged black men to enlist. In the navy, black men were not just cook's assistants and stewards but they served as gunners and helmsmen.

In peacetime, many black men had been sailors working aboard merchantmen, whalers, and coastal ships. They had the skill and experience that sailors needed. When the war started, every ship that could be fitted for war duty was sent to sea. These ships needed crews and the navy took everyone who volunteered. Soon, one man in three in the U.S. Navy was black. There were no black officers, however. The navy chiefs would not go that far.

"Well, that's the navy," the army men said. "We can't have black soldiers."

Why not? Black men had fought as soldiers in all the wars of colonial times. There were 5,000 black men in Washington's Army during the American Revolution. Black men had fought at New Orleans with Andrew Jackson in the War of 1812. Each time, they fought bravely, and well. Why couldn't they fight now?

President Lincoln and the War Department kept saying no.

Behind that "no" was the bitter question of slavery, the question that divided the country. The question that had to be settled—even in the midst of war—forever.

2 The Emancipation Proclamation

For many years there had been a group of people in the North who hated slavery. They called themselves *abolitionists* because they wanted to *abolish*, to do away with, slavery. Some abolitionists were whites and some were free blacks. All of them hated slavery and were determined to get rid of it. They wrote strong words against slavery and they spoke out against it everywhere they could.

Their most famous speaker was Frederick Douglass. He, like many other black men, through his own courage had fled from slavery. Now he wanted black men to fight their way to freedom. To fight the South without using black soldiers, Douglass said, was to fight with one arm tied behind the Union's back.

The abolitionists believed not only that there should be black troops, but that black troops should have black officers.

Governor John Andrew of Massachusetts agreed. The governor too was a staunch fighter against slavery. Since the beginning of the war he had wanted to use black men as fighting soldiers. He was eager to recruit a black regiment right in his own state of Massachusetts. Time and again he wrote to President Lincoln about it, without success.

But the war was going badly for the North, and this forced the President to reconsider. So, in June

John A. Andrew
Governor of Massachusetts
1860-1866

17

1862, the War Department said a few black men could be organized into special combat units.

Most of those who joined up in these units were runaway slaves from Louisiana and South Carolina. These men had fled to territory held by Union armies and worked there as laborers. When the chance came to become soldiers, they hurried to sign up. Several regiments were formed. They were known as the *Corps d'Afrique*—the African troops. Their officers were white.

The abolitionists did not believe it was enough that a few men had been enrolled in the Corps d'Afrique. They kept calling for the widespread use of black soldiers. For a long time, they met with no further success.

Then came the Second Battle of Bull Run, fought near Manassas, Virginia. The battle was a terrible defeat for the North. The Union troops had been poorly led and the losses were frightful. The defeat was so bad that it all but dried up the trickle of volunteers that had been joining the Union Army.

At this time the President had an important statement to make. A statement that, for many, would change the whole meaning of the war. Lincoln's advisers suggested that he wait until the North won a battle before he make his announcement.

A section of the Emancipation Proclamation in Abraham Lincoln's own handwriting.

And I hereby enjoin upon the people so declared to be free to abstain from all violence, unless in necessary self-defence; and I recommend to them that in all cases when allowed, they labor faithfully for reasonable wages.

And I further declare and make known, that such persons of suitable condition, will be received into the armed service of the United States to garrison forts, positions stations, and other places, and to man vessels of all sorts in said service.

And upon this act, sincerely believed to be an act of justice, warranted by the Constitution, upon military necessity, I invoke the considerate judgment of mankind, and the gracious favor of Almighty God.

In witness whereof I have hereunto set my hand and caused the seal of the United States to be affixed.

Done at the city of Washington, this first day of January, in the year of our Lord one thousand eight hundred and sixty three, and of

Soon after Bull Run, another great battle took place. On September 17, 1862, General Robert E. Lee led his Confederate Army out of Virginia and invaded the North. Yanks and Rebels met and fought in Maryland, on the banks of Antietam Creek. In a bloody battle and at great cost, the North forced Lee back into Virginia. Great as the losses of the North were, Lincoln was encouraged. Antietam seemed to be a northern victory. So, Lincoln made his announcement—it was his plan for an Emancipation Proclamation.

In this statement Lincoln declared that after January 1, 1863, *all slaves in territory held by the Rebels would be forever free.*

If the Confederates stopped fighting *before* January 1, they could keep their slaves.

What about slaves in the loyal border states? These slaves were not freed. What about slaves in areas held by Union troops. They were not included either. Lincoln did not believe the Constitution gave him the power to free them.

The proclamation was intended to help win the war. The President and his advisers hoped that it would greatly weaken the South. Lincoln hoped that when slaves heard they were free, they would run away from their owners by the thousands.

The southern leaders knew this could not happen. They laughed at the Proclamation. Lincoln was a fool, they said. How could he sit in Washington and declare black people in Alabama free?

The abolitionists hailed the Proclamation. No, it didn't go far enough, they said. The government should have ordered *all slaves, everywhere in the country*, to be set free. But the Emancipation Proclamation gave the promise of freedom. It was a step in the right direction.

By this time there were many more abolitionists. But there were also many in the North who did not like Lincoln's new position on slavery.

"We're supposed to be fighting to preserve the Union," they said. "We don't intend to spill our blood for black people!"

Lincoln knew that these people in the North were against him. But he met their criticism calmly.

On January 1, 1863, the Emancipation Proclamation became law.

As Lincoln had hoped, it gave many the heart to keep fighting. It swung the people of France and England to the support of the Union. And of course it made both slaves and free black people shout for joy. Slavery was doomed. And very important for the North was one sentence from the Emancipation Proclamation. The sentence that said black men could now be "received into the armed service of the United States."

3 "You Belong in the 54th!"

GOVERNOR JOHN ANDREW was the first governor in the North to start raising black troops. The regiment was to be called the 54th Massachusetts Volunteers, and the governor meant to see that it was a model unit. However, Governor Andrew was met with an immediate disappointment. The War Department said the commissioned officers of the 54th had to be white! The corporals and sergeants could be black. Governor Andrew protested sharply to the War Department. This was unfair. Other people supported his protest. But the Secretary of War was firm. All the officers from lieutenant to colonel had to be white. If they were not, the regiment would not be allowed to fight.

"Very well," said Governor Andrew. But he had

made an important decision. He would go through the entire Massachusetts list and pick out the best and bravest men. They would be officers who had proved themselves in battle. What's more, he would call only for such men who had shown their sympathy for black people by word and deed!

Who would be the colonel to command the 54th? The governor went over the list very carefully, and then set his mind on Robert Gould Shaw. Shaw was a captain in the 2nd Massachusetts Volunteers. He was twenty-four years old, a Harvard University graduate. In his two years of duty he had seen a lot of action. Shaw was the son of an abolitionist, and Governor Andrew was sure he was the right man.

To the governor's surprise and disappointment, Robert Shaw turned down the offer to be the colonel of the 54th. "I am flattered," the young captain wrote, "that you believe me worthy of leading black men into battle. . . . It is indeed an honor. . . . But I do not think myself qualified to accept. . . ."

Shaw had turned the offer down, but after he had done so, he felt sick at heart. He was a man used to looking deep into himself. He knew why he had said no, and he was not proud of the reason. He was afraid that he would be looked down upon if he entered a black regiment. He said as much to some of his fellow officers.

"But you were absolutely right to refuse," some of them told him. "Stay where you *belong*."

Robert Gould Shaw, 1837-1863
Commander of the 54th Massachusetts Volunteers

"After all, Bob," one of his friends said, "it's one thing to feel sorry for blacks and another to rub shoulders with them. Let Andrew pick another colonel, a man who's not a gentleman such as you."

In spite of what his friends said, Shaw was ashamed of the reason he had turned the governor down. When he learned that Captain Norwood Hallowell had snapped up the chance to be second in command of the black regiment, Shaw felt even worse. Hallowell was just as educated, just as rich, and just as much a gentleman as himself.

Robert Shaw took another close look at why he had refused. Then he wrote to Annie Haggerty. She was the beautiful New York girl he was going to marry. He wanted her to know what he had done and why. "To my own shame," he wrote in his letter, "I now see I dreaded what people would say about my entering the Negro regiment. I was thinking of you as well as myself. You will soon be my bride. I could not bear for you to suffer because of me."

Shaw thought he knew Annie Haggerty. But he didn't at all. She was shocked by his letter. Instead of answering it, Annie took the train to Alexandria, Virginia, where the young captain was in winter quarters. She was a fiery abolitionist and could not trust herself to put down on paper what she felt.

Annie had to say what was on her mind, and say it in person to her future husband.

"Robert," she said, "you are not to worry about me. You have to do what is right—and that's all. When black men go into battle, they must be commanded by men who are not prejudiced against them. They must be led by men like you, not by men who would enter a black regiment just because it meant promotion for them. Robert, you *belong* with the 54th. There lies your fate and mine!"

How happy Shaw felt to hear this from Annie! His friends had urged him to stay where he "belonged." But Annie had shown him that he "belonged" with the 54th. This was where he wanted to be. Immediately he sent Governor Andrew a telegram: "Disregard my letter. It will be my privilege to command the 54th Massachusetts Volunteers if the post is still open."

Governor Andrew sent a return telegram to Shaw saying that his name had been sent on to the War Department. The governor was asking that Robert Gould Shaw be granted a temporary commission as colonel in the U.S. Volunteers.

By the middle of February 1863, the transfer had been made. With a colonel's eagles on his shoulders instead of a captain's bars, Shaw was in Boston, getting the recruiting started.

When other officers heard that Shaw would command the 54th, they rushed to join the regiment. Shaw had set an example. Others wanted to follow in his footsteps. It became an honor to belong to the 54th not only because it was black, but because Robert Shaw was its commander.

What can be said of these other white officers? All of them were young—the average age was 23— yet 14 had already been in battle. Many were men well-educated, wealthy, and well-known in New York, Boston, and Philadelphia. Though not all the 29 officers were abolitionists, most had strong anti-slavery feelings, and were eager to serve in a black regiment.

4 Putting Flesh on the Bones

THE OFFICERS of the 54th were everything the governor could have wished for, but so far, the regiment itself existed only on paper. Soldiers had to be recruited. It was soon clear that a full regiment of black soldiers could not possibly be raised in Massachusetts alone. At most, Massachusetts could count on getting 394 men. Boston raised one company and New Bedford another. But in the whole state there were simply not enough black men of military age to form a regiment. It also became clear that a full regiment could not even be raised in all of New England. Maine, Vermont, New Hampshire, Rhode Island, and Connecticut simply did not have large enough populations of black people to draw from.

Governor Andrew was not discouraged. He called on his old friend George Stearns. Stearns was a rich man and an active abolitionist. He had helped John Brown raise the money for his raid on Harper's Ferry. Now Governor Andrew asked him to help recruit black soldiers for the 54th.

Stearns got right to work. He organized a group of people to help him. One member of the group was Francis G. Shaw, the colonel's father. All were abolitionists.

"What we need," the group decided, "is to let people know. Let's get money together for leaflets and posters. Let's put up notices in every part of the country. Let's advertise in the newspapers."

In Massachusetts, daily newspapers ran ads like this:

TO COLORED MEN:
Wanted! Good men for the 54th regiment of Massachusetts Volunteers of Africa Descent. Colonel Robert Gould Shaw, commanding. $100 bounty at expiration of term of service. Pay $13 a month and State aid for families. All necessary information can be obtained at the office, Corner Cambridge and North Russell Streets.

Lieut. J. W. M. Appleton
Recruiting Officer

Stearns did not stop with newspaper ads. They were just the beginning. Because he was a well-

Henry Highland Garnet, 1815-1882
Chaplain of black regiments during
Civil War. Minister to Liberia, 1881.

known abolitionist, Stearns knew nearly all of the black men in the country who were fighting for their people. He asked them to help. He hired Martin Delany, John and Charles Langston, O. S. B. Wall, Henry Highland Garnet, Henry M. Turner, and others. Many of these men felt that fighting in this war would force white people to treat black people with fairness.

Stearns was especially glad to get help from Frederick Douglass. More than any of the other

William Lloyd Garrison, 1805-1879
Abolitionist, editor, and publisher
of the *Liberator*.

John M. Langston, 1829-1897
Black abolitionist, Congressman,
and author.

black men, Douglass felt that black men could fight
their way to citizenship.

His own sons, Lewis and Charles, were the first
black men from New York State to join the 54th
Massachusetts. Douglass had a warm spot in his
heart for the regiment and he was only too happy
to help recruit. He traveled all over the North speaking to black men. He told them that the time had
come. Strong black arms must now tear down the
slave owner's house.

"We can get at the throat of treason and slavery through Massachusetts," he said. "She was first in the War of Independence; first to break the chains of her slaves; first to make the black man equal before the law; first to admit colored children to her common schools. . . . Massachusetts now welcomes you as her soldiers."

Stearn's agents roamed far in their search for black soldiers. Recruiting stations were set up in all parts of the East and as far west as Chicago.

Many slaves had fled from the United States to Canada. Helped by the Underground Railroad, they were now free men. None hated slavery more than those men who had fled it, who had gone so far with only friends and the North Star to guide them.

The appeal to black men outside Massachusetts brought immediate results. Men who had faced the dangers and the terrible hardships of the flight from slavery left their homes in Canada. They came back to fight their former owners.

But even as the volunteers poured in, there were voices that cried, "A black regiment? It will never work out!"

"The whole idea is wrong," said a Union Army officer. "They'll run at the first shot!"

There were many people in the North who wanted the South to win. These people were called *Copperheads*—the name of a poisonous snake. The Copperheads hated President Lincoln, and they attacked him cruelly in their newspapers. The editor of the

Frederick Douglass, 1817-1895

New York *Daily News* was one person who couldn't stand the idea of using black men as soldiers. "What evil would Lincoln thrust upon us next?" he wrote. "That man Lincoln would do anything to win the support of the ignorant blacks!"

People who were against the idea of a black regiment didn't fight with words alone. They did everything they could to stop the recruiting of the 54th Volunteers. Gangs hung around the recruiting stations and tried to scare off the recruiting officers.

Lieutenant James W. Grace, who set up an office in New Bedford, Massachusetts, had all he could do to keep it open. Gangs threw rocks at the windows of his headquarters and attacked men coming to enlist. After a while Lieutenant Grace had to carry a gun.

"I vow to shoot down the next Copperhead attempting to hinder me at my legal and authorized duty!" he said.

But the attacks went on until Governor Andrew posted an armed guard at the New Bedford recruiting station.

The men who wanted to enlist were not frightened away. However, not every man who wanted to be a soldier was taken. Many were turned down because they couldn't pass the medical exam. This exam was harder to pass than usual, harder than the physical test given to white soldiers. The doctor in charge, Surgeon Lincoln R. Stone, kept saying, "We want only perfect men. Our lads will be physically and mentally fit for combat." The men of the 54th could not be *good*—they had to be *best*. The eyes of the nation were on them.

The surgeons kept weeding men out. But so many men offered themselves that the regiment kept growing. Finally—nine hundred men had passed the difficult medical test. The 54th regiment was complete. The recruiting stations could close their doors.

5 They Stepped Out with Pride

Even as the 54th was being recruited, training quarters for the regiment had to be made ready. For the time being, the men were to be housed at the Armory in Boston. But they would get their training at Camp Meigs, in a little town called Readville, a few miles south of Boston.

The officers of the 54th knew Camp Meigs well. It was the camp where they had done their own basic training. So Lieutenant Colonel Norwood Hallowell felt a little as if he were going home when, with a group of men from the 54th, he boarded the train to Readville. It was March 1863; Hallowell and his men were on their way to Camp Meigs to inspect the regiment's quarters.

In his mind's eye, Hallowell saw the camp as it had looked when he trained there. He recalled how the oaks and elms, and beech and poplar trees had made a bright and cheerful background for the well-kept buildings.

When they arrived at Camp Meigs, the skies were gray and rain threatened. Though it was March, it was cold. The trees were still bare and the ground was frozen mud. Most disheartening of all were the quarters that had been assigned to the 54th. When Hallowell looked at the barracks they had been given, he flushed with anger. They were the worst in the place!

The men looked around at the gloomy and long neglected barracks, at the broken windows, sagging roofs, and peeling walls. They saw supply sheds and mess halls in equally bad shape. Was this the same Camp Meigs that Lieutenant Hallowell had told them about?

But no one grumbled. There was no time for complaining. The 54th was supposed to leave Boston for Camp Meigs on March 14!

"Never mind, men," said Hallowell, trying to sound more cheerful than he felt. "I'll wire Colonel Shaw to send a crew here at once, so we can get this place in shape before our troops arrive. Back in the Boston Armory, the 54th has men who can do everything that needs to be done here."

When Colonel Shaw received word from Hallowell, he turned to Governor Andrew for help. There was nothing the governor wouldn't get if the 54th needed it.

Lumber, paint, pipes, and tools were rushed out to Camp Meigs. A work crew of men from the regiment—carpenters, stone masons, plumbers, housepainters, and plasterers—arrived almost immediately. Soon the noise of hammers and saws resounded through the camp. Before many days had passed, the 54th had the neatest quarters in Camp Meigs.

Back in Boston, Colonel Shaw was busy all day long. Food, clothing, weapons, and ammunition had to be shipped to the camp. Sheets, blankets, medical supplies, and a thousand and one other things had to be taken care of. Last minute problems kept coming up. Nevertheless, at the time set, the enlisted men and the officers of the 54th Massachusetts Volunteers marched from the Armory to the railroad station.

The men carried no arms. Though they were wearing their uniforms, they were not yet soldiers. They felt self-conscious in their stiff new clothes, but they stepped out with pride. People stopped to watch the men go by.

At the station, a special train was waiting to take the recruits to Readville. On the station plaform, the band was playing "Rally 'Round the Flag!" Friends and relatives of the soldiers crowded around to see them off. There was laughter. There were also tears. These men were going off to be trained for war.

Exactly at noon, the engine whistle shrieked,

steam hissed, smoke and sparks belched from the stack, and the train moved away. Good-bye! Good-bye!

Two hours later, the men of the 54th got off the train at Readville. Small groups of townspeople watched them with stony faces. Readville had never seen black troops before. What would they be like?

The men had to hike nearly five miles to Camp Meigs. But nobody minded—the day was balmy, not a cloud in the sky, the sunshine bright. "It's a good omen," Shaw wrote to Annie Haggerty that night. "This has been the first pleasant day we've had for weeks."

There were no radios, telephones, or television when the Civil War broke out. News of the war spread by telegraph, newspapers, leaflets, billboards.

LATEST FROM
CHARLESTON
—
SUMTER ON FIRE!!
REBELS FIRING ON
THE BURNING FORT!!

Scene around a billboard in the North.

THE

UNION
IS
DISSOLVED!

MERCURY

EXTRA:

Passed unanimously at 1.15 o'clock, P. M., December 20th, 1860.

AN ORDINANCE

To dissolve the Union between the State of South Carolina and other States united with her under the compact entitled "The Constitution of the United States of America."

We, the People of the State of South Carolina, in Convention assembled, do declare and ordain, and it is hereby declared and ordained,

That the Ordinance adopted by us in Convention, on the twenty-third day of May, in the year of our Lord one thousand seven hundred and eighty-eight, whereby the Constitution of the United States of America was ratified, and also, all Acts and parts of Acts of the General Assembly of this State, ratifying amendments of the said Constitution, are hereby repealed; and that the union now subsisting between South Carolina and other States, under the name of "The United States of America," is hereby dissolved.

The South gets news that war has started.

A poster calling for men to volunteer for the Union Army.

Montgomery, Alabama, on the day Jefferson Davis was sworn in as President of the Confederate States.

Slaves building a fort for the Confederacy. Even free blacks were forced to work for the South.

Captured Confederate soldiers.

A black man working for the Union as a cook.

Black women working as washwomen for the Union.

Slaves left behind by their owner when he fled to escape the Union troops. Abandoned slaves sometimes stayed on the plantations where they had worked. But most went along with the Union soldiers. These slaves with the Union Army were called *contraband of war*.

A newspaper cartoon showing a slave holding up the Confederacy. It was slave labor that freed white men to fight.

A wagon train of runaway slaves crossing the Rappahannock River in Virginia.

A newspaper cartoon showing slaves running away to Fort Monroe. General Ben Butler was in command of that fort, and he was the first to call the runaways "contraband."

General Ben Butler welcoming runaway slaves.

Black volunteers line up outside a recruiting office.

The ring leaders of the mob.

A lynching.

Scenes from the New York City draft riots of 1863.

Burning an orphan asylum.

Mob scenes.

6 "A Remarkable Body of Men"

Camp Meigs was a little world of its own, but like the world outside, it was full of white people who did not like black people. Many white soldiers were also getting their training at Camp Meigs, and at first they were rude and insulting to the black men. Every time a unit of the 54th appeared on the drill field or rifle range, the whites jeered. But very quickly the 54th began to "shape up." Within two weeks the jeering stopped.

"I must tell you that I've been wrong about the black regiment here, the 54th," a white soldier wrote home. "I used to think that blacks were a shiftless lot. But this is as fine a bunch of men as you'd ever hope to see. Real friendly fellows too, when you give them half a chance and get to know them. I don't reckon I'll think the same about blacks again."

Many other white soldiers would never think the same of blacks again after the War Department reported on the first black troops in battle. The Corps d'Afrique had fought the rebels in the South. No, the blacks had not "run at the first shot" as people had said they would. Few white troops had behaved so well under fire for the first time. In one encounter the blacks had routed the Rebels.

Some of this glory rubbed off on the 54th, and at Camp Meigs, the white troops now looked at the regiment in a new light. After all, these white troops had not yet "seen the elephant," as the men called being under fire for the first time. How would they behave when the time came? Would they run? Would the 54th be the ones to push the Rebels back, as those first black troops had done?

The white soldiers at Camp Meigs had to admit that Colonel Shaw's troops were showing themselves to be able soldiers. Their discipline was the best at Camp Meigs. Everybody knew that among the white troops there were many cases of disobedience. Soldiers often got drunk and were disorderly. In the 54th Massachusetts there was almost no trouble of this kind.

Not that all the men in the 54th were well behaved. Some of the recruits did not like army life. They had been free men, and independent.

Many had risked death to escape from slavery because they wanted no master. Here, in the army, they were told how to stand, when to sit, where to go, what to do. The discipline was strict and not everyone would take it. But the number who broke the rules was far less than that in white regiments at Camp Meigs.

Perhaps no one was more pleased about the report on the Corps d'Afrique than was Colonel Shaw. It was also good news to him too that commanders in the field were now *asking* for black troops. Some of these officers had sworn they would resign before accepting black troops. Now they were bombarding the War Department with requests.

Colonel Shaw did not doubt that the 54th would behave well under fire. But Shaw wouldn't be satisfied if his men merely did well. When their turn came to "see the elephant," he wanted the 54th regiment to do even better than those first troops that had won so much praise.

Shaw knew that troops often lost battles and suffered many losses because they were poorly trained. "The 54th is going into combat fully prepared," he told an aide. "Our men will know what to do when they reach the front."

Shaw laid down a schedule for his regiment that other troops would have rebelled against. But the 54th took it and liked it. They didn't need to be driven—they drove themselves.

People who came to visit the camp noticed this too. They were always impressed by the spirit of the 54th. One day a reporter from Boston was talking to Sergeant Major Lewis Douglass, a son of Frederick Douglass.

"The black troops seem to be more zealous than the white troops at Camp Meigs," the reporter remarked. "If you had been regarded as nothing more than a beast of burden all your life," said Lewis Douglass, "and then got the chance to be a man would you not be more zealous than others?"

The reporter nodded. "I think I understand."

Shaw pushed his men hard, but seldom had any commander had troops so eager to learn the business of soldiering. They learned how to assault and hold a position; to dig in; to attack in column, platoon, and company front. They learned cover and concealment; fire and movement; how to use bayonet and rifle butt. They were taught scouting, patroling, and to march at night. A great deal of time was spent on the rifle range and most of the men became good shots.

Colonel Shaw felt he had the right to be proud of the 54th, and he wanted to share his feeling with Governor Andrew. Who would understand the colonel's pride as well as the governor? Was he not as much a part of the 54th as Shaw?

When the black troops had been at Camp Meigs six weeks the colonel sent the governor a report:

"Everything goes well for us. The intelligence of

the men is high. Their devotion to duty knows no bounds. They have learned soldiering more readily than most. There is no doubt that we shall leave the state with as good a regiment as any which has marched since the outbreak of the war."

This was less than Shaw really felt. What he wanted to say, but was too modest, was that the 54th would be the *best* regiment that had marched out of the state since the outbreak of the war.

The men of the 54th were robust, strong, and healthy, and it was no wonder. The regiment's surgeons set up rigid health rules. And the men were willing to obey them.

Army doctors knew pretty well what should be done at any camp to preserve health. But it was one thing to *say* what should be done and another to see that it *was* done. At Camp Meigs, some outfits paid little attention to rules. Latrines were put in the wrong places—often so close to places where drinking water came from that sewage got into the water. Food was badly cared for, and became spoiled, still it was served to the men. The men didn't bathe. Regiments that were careless about health regulations were hit hard by illness, and the death rates in these outfits was high. The health record of the 54th was excellent. The black regiment's area was the cleanest at Camp Meigs.

In the 54th, the company kitchens were spotless. Foods that might spoil were stored in ice chests. Latrines were dug very deep and were placed far from supplies of drinking water. The barracks were given a thorough cleaning every week. And they were inspected every single day. Captain Appleton, commander of Company A, wore white gloves when he went on morning inspection. He would poke his fingers into corners, and if the glove came out smudged, he "raised hell."

Colonel Shaw's men were strong and healthy and proud that they had the best health record in camp.

"We aim to be the finest regiment in the whole army!" a black soldier wrote home. "And we're going to do it!"

7 Colors for the 54th

THE 54TH did not get to be a top-notch unit without great effort all around. Shaw and his staff stayed up late every evening preparing for the next day's training. No detail was neglected, no weakness was passed over. The officers pushed hard, and the men gave all they had.

As a result the 54th became a famous regiment. Hardly a week went by without its being called upon to drill before congressmen, senators, or other important people.

The men had worked hard to be best. And they liked showing how good they were. The regimental band would sound off with a snappy marching tune, and the troops would pass in review, the men stepping out exactly in line.

But it was not just the splendid way they looked or their perfect marching order that impressed spectators. There was something *inside* the men that came through. A Massachusetts state senator expressed it when he said, "These are the proudest soldiers I have ever seen!"

Sergeant William Carney, a man from New Bedford, later recalled how he and his comrades felt about being soldiers in the 54th: "Nothing any of us had ever done before was as important as this. We were fighting for all black men and could not fail." They were acting out what Frederick Douglass had said to the black men of Rochester, New York: "Liberty won by white men would lose half its luster. Who would be free must themselves strike the blow. Better even to die free than to live slaves. . . ."

Each man of the 54th felt this. Each marched as though he were marching for all black people.

In May, Colonel Shaw reported to Governor Andrew: "I believe we are now ready to carry out any mission."

Governor Andrew was pleased. He was already recruiting a second black regiment, the 55th Massachusetts Volunteers. Norwood Hallowell would

A poster calling for black men to join the army. It is signed by many black leaders.

MEN OF COLOR

To Arms! To Arms!

NOW OR NEVER

THREE YEARS' SERVICE!

BATTLES OF LIBERTY AND THE UNION

FAIL NOW, & OUR RACE IS DOOMED

SILENCE THE TONGUE OF CALUMNY

VALOR AND HEROISM

PORT HUDSON AND MILLIKEN'S BEND.

ARE FREEMEN LESS BRAVE THAN SLAVES

OUR LAST OPPORTUNITY HAS COME

MEN OF COLOR, BROTHERS AND FATHERS!

WE APPEAL TO YOU!

STRIKE NOW!

command this unit. The 55th would go into training when the 54th left Camp Meigs.

That time was drawing near. . . .

On Monday, May 18, 1863, streams of visitors poured into Camp Meigs. They were coming to see an important event. The 54th Massachusetts Volunteers were "graduating." The regiment was going to receive its colors. After this, the 54th would become a fighting unit.

Governor Andrew and the mayor of Boston were there. So were the famous anti-slavery fighters Wendell Phillips, William Lloyd Garrison, and Frederick Douglass. Many other important people came too, among them merchants, bankers, and professional people who had served on the Stearns Committee. And mingling with the rich and the well-known were the parents, friends, wives, and sweethearts of the soldiers.

The men were all keyed up. Reveille had sounded at 5 A.M. that morning, 45 minutes earlier than usual. After gulping breakfast, they had set to work polishing brass, shining shoes, cleaning weapons, and sprucing up their barracks and grounds.

Every man's spirit was high as each company in the regiment moved to the drill field and massed in parade formation. Three officers from other Massachusetts regiments carried to Governor Andrew three furled flags. One by one the governor handed the flags to Colonel Shaw—a state flag, a national flag, and a regimental flag. In turn, Shaw passed the banners on to the color bearers of the 54th.

The flag bearers unfurled the banners. Then they marched back into place at the center of the regimental formation. The three flags waved in the breeze, revealing the design of the regimental colors: On a red background was a figure of the Goddess of Liberty surrounded by the words *Liberty*, *Unity*, and *Loyalty*. Across the bottom of the silk flag was embroidered a motto in Latin: *In hoc signo vinces*, meaning *You conquer in this sign*.

When the flag bearers were back in place, Governor Andrew made a speech. Then, Frederick Douglass and several other people addressed the 54th. Colonel Shaw replied for the regiment.

He said little, but his words were heartfelt:

"We vow to defend these colors with our lives," he said. "We shall cherish and protect them under every circumstance. Not without honor do we accept these flags that you place in our keeping. You shall never regret your faith in us."

He nodded to the band. The musicians struck up a lively air. The companies wheeled smartly into line, color bearers and guard in front, and paraded snappily past the governor. As the colors were dipped before him, Governor Andrew took the salute.

It was a stirring sight, and few eyes were dry, as the colors were carried by. Then the unexpected happened. The parade was still going on when a rider galloped up to Governor Andrew and handed

Major General David Hunter, 1802-1866

him a telegram. The governor opened the envelope, read the message, and passed it on to Colonel Shaw, who stood beside him.

As he read the wire, the young colonel smiled. He waited till the march past ended and the troops were drawn up in company front. Then he strode out to face the 54th, and in a voice that carried to the farthest ranks, he announced:

"Men! I have a telegram from the War Department ordering this regiment to report to General David Hunter, Commanding Officer, Department of the South, for combat duty in South Carolina. This order is effective at once!"

For a moment there was silence. Then a great cheer went up. Caps went sailing in the air. The men broke ranks, and pounded one another on the back. The excitement quickly spread to the onlookers. Everybody joined in. Black and white cheered together.

For the time being no one was thinking of the perils that awaited the 54th in the war zone—of the men, now so happily cheering, who might soon be dead, or maimed, or blinded. In that exciting moment, something else was important.

The men of the 54th were realizing their deepest wish. They were about to go into battle—at last—in the war against slavery.

8 Off to the War

ONCE THE ORDERS had come to move into the war zone, training became more intense than ever. The men of the 54th were up at the crack of dawn and they never stopped going until after dark. Sometimes they even held maneuvers at night.

On May 26, 1863, Colonel Shaw was informed that in two days his regiment was to sail south from Boston aboard the transport steamer *De Molay*.

At 6 A.M. on May 28, the regiment stood in line ready for the long march to the Readville railroad station. Bands played and flags waved as the black soldiers marched off along the dusty road to town. Other units in the camp had come out to bid the

54th good-bye. White soldiers saluted as the black soldiers stepped out smartly. Color guards of other regiments dipped their banners to the blacks. The bands struck up patriotic airs.

At Readville a special train was waiting on the tracks, its locomotive already huffing. The men got aboard shouting farewell to the townspeople who had gathered to see them off. The citizens of Readville were proud of the 54th too. Women came over to the train windows and handed the men bags of cookies. Men passed out cigars and tobacco to the soldiers. "They're setting out to do God's work," one citizen said, and took off his hat. Many a silent prayer went up for the safe return of the departing soldiers.

But the send-off at Readville was only a foretaste of the reception awaiting the 54th in Boston. When at 9 o'clock the train pulled into Boston's North Station, thousands of people lined the streets.

From North Station the soldiers marched to the State House and Boston Common. Mounted city police led the march. Behind them came Colonel Shaw on a magnificent white horse. The regiment followed, its color guard in front, sunlight glinting on the spear points of the flags they carried.

That gala day, blacks and whites mingled in a spirit of brotherhood and good will. Police struggled to hold back the crowd while girls tossed flowers at the marching soldiers. Bands played. The Stars and Stripes flew from every house. Every window, balcony, and rooftop along the way was jammed with cheering people.

The cheering never stopped. Many a regiment had marched through Boston, but never had soldiers been received like this. Even as they cheered, many onlookers wiped tears from their eyes. No one was ashamed to cry.

On the steps of the State House, Shaw's parents stood among the spectators. As the regiment approached and Shaw's mother saw the colonel riding at the front, her eyes filled. "What have I done that God is so good to me?" she murmured. How proud she was of her son, how proud that he was riding at the head of a *black* regiment, leading men who knew so well what they were fighting for.

The beautiful girl who had been Annie Haggerty stood with the Shaws. The colonel and his sweetheart had been married two weeks before, and she was now Annie Shaw. She stood there joyously waving a small American flag, her face wet with happy tears.

From the reviewing stand at one end of Boston Common, Governor Andrew addressed the troops. He was followed by abolitionist Wendell Phillips who bade the blacks godspeed.

Then Frederick Douglass spoke: "My brothers," he said, "you are going off to fight the slavemasters. When you are in battle remember the shame, the disgrace, the degradation of slavery! Remember, that in your strong hands is held the salvation of

62

the black people of America. For once you have spent your blood, no black man will ever again be enslaved. I am too old to go with you. But my sons are in your ranks. Go into battle boldly, my brothers! Smash the chains of slavery! Smash them!" Douglass turned, choked with emotion. Then, he cried, "God bless you all!"

When the speeches were over, the officers of the 54th and their guests were invited into the State House, where a grand luncheon awaited them, while the troops were called to a buffet lunch on the Common. There long wooden tables were set out. The tables were heaped high with cold meats, potato salad, pies, cakes, fruit, coffee, and lemonade. Soldiers, wives, sweethearts, relatives, and friends helped themselves generously. The food never seemed to give out! All of it had been prepared by a group of Boston women, black and white, who called themselves "Friends of the 54th Massachusetts Volunteers."

It was half past two when the luncheon in the State House was over. Colonel Shaw parted tenderly from his wife and parents. The officers reported to their companies. A bugler blew "Assembly." The soldiers shook hands with relatives and friends and kissed their wives and sweethearts good-bye. The regiment marched to Battery Wharf, where the *De Molay* rode at anchor.

Huge crowds stood on the wharf, watching as company by company the troops filed aboard the

transport. At last the whole regiment was aboard—
with horses, baggage, and all. The steam whistle
shrieked. Somewhere on the pier a band began playing "Auld Lang Syne." Slowly the *De Molay* nosed
out while the throng on shore cheered and waved
flags. From where they stood at the railings, the
soldiers shouted back to the people.

Slowly the ship turned, her prow pointing south,
and headed for the open sea. The 54th Massachusetts was off to the war.

9 "We Can Count on the Colonel in a Pinch."

THE *De Molay* was a new steamer of the latest design, a clean, well-lighted ship. The officers shared light, airy staterooms and ate their meals in a splendid dining room. The quarters for the enlisted men were not as good, but the troops were comfortable, and the food was good and plentiful.

Few of the men aboard the *De Molay* had ever been on an ocean-going vessel before. Luckily the weather was fine all the way to South Carolina.

On the second of June, the ship dropped anchor outside the harbor of Charleston. Some twenty other Union craft were anchored there—warships, merchantmen, and transports. Were the U.S. Navy vessels gathered there for an attack on Charleston? It was at Charleston that the rebellion had started, and the town was still held by the Confederates.

Charleston was a city besieged, but strongly defended. It would be very costly to take. Nevertheless, it was rumored that the U.S. Army was planning to attack Charleston and that the 54th would take part. The men were excited by the thought of seeing action. Then suddenly on the afternoon of the third of June, the *De Molay* hauled anchor and sailed to Beaufort on the island of Port Royal. Now, the regiment was sixty miles south of Charleston. Nobody seemed to know why.

Next day, at 5 o'clock in the morning, the regiment debarked. The little town of Beaufort was still sleeping as the blacks marched through. The men marched four or five miles to the abandoned plantation which was to be their camp. As soon as they saw it, they realized they were in for a bad time.

The ground was boggy. There were no tents. The ration wagons did not arrive. And it drizzled all the time. Worst of all were the mosquitoes. They seemed to be the biggest and fiercest mosquitoes in the world. The men had a saying that six mosquitoes could drag away a horse.

For four days the men suffered, encamped on this mosquito-infested bog. Most of the time they had nothing to eat except hardtack and black coffee. Stationed near them were two regiments of U.S.

Colored Troops, as the Corps d'Afrique were now called.

Colonel Shaw and his staff set off to find out if there wasn't a better place for the 54th to camp. The colonel came back in a rage. He had discovered that the white troops were stationed in an excellent place. No bog, no mosquitoes. What was more, there was plenty of room available in the same area. Only the 54th and U.S. Colored Troops had been sent off to camp on a mosquito-ridden swamp.

Shaw protested angrily to the sector commander. But no attention was paid to his complaint.

"Forget it," the commander of one of the colored regiments said to Shaw. "You won't get anywhere with him. He can't stand the idea of black soldiers. We just have to take it."

Colonel Shaw refused to "take it." He sent a wire to Governor Andrew. Andrew immediately got in touch with the Secretary of War. "I will recall the 54th unless the situation is corrected at once," the governor threatened. The 54th had not yet been sworn into federal service, so the regiment was still under state control.

The Secretary of War didn't want to lose the famous 54th. He acted promptly. Suddenly there were supplies for the 54th—tents, cots, rations. Indeed the quartermaster sent enough supplies for a brigade, let alone for a regiment! These were supplies he had had all the time, but had withheld from the black troops.

The men of the 54th understood very clearly what was happening. They saw too that they could trust Colonel Shaw to act on their behalf. "We can count on him," they said. In spite of everything, therefore, the spirit of the men remained high.

On June 6, Shaw received orders to leave Beaufort two days later. The 54th was sent to St. Simon's Island, located a few miles off the coast of Georgia.

Lieutenant Colonel Edward Hallowell called the island "a Garden of Eden." Flowers, trees, and birds were everywhere. The beaches were wonderful for swimming. The camp quarters assigned to the 54th were almost perfect. With tents, cots, field kitchens, and plentiful rations, everybody was happy.

The day after the 54th arrived on St. Simon's Island, the regiment was sworn into federal service. It was made part of a brigade together with the 1st and 2nd South Carolina—the U.S. Colored Troops from Beaufort. The commander of the brigade was General James Montgomery.

Free-born blacks, contraband, and newly escaped slaves
stood in recruitment lines in the winter of 1863.

On picket duty.

A dress parade.

A black regiment receiving its colors. Each regiment was given a flag, or banner, having colors different from any other regiment's colors.

A black color guard.

The camp of black soldiers stationed on James Island, South Carolina.

Black soldiers going off to the battlefront to fight against slavery.

In the Army, black and white foot soldiers had the same duties. They stood on picket, they drilled, they practiced firing, and much more. But, on payday, each white soldier received thirteen dollars — each black received seven.

10 "Burn the Village Down!"

GENERAL MONTGOMERY hailed from Kansas. He was a rough man—a tough fighter. More important, he had powerful friends in the War Department. His skill and his friends had gotten him his command.

Colonel Shaw saw immediately that General Montgomery was trouble with a capital T. He was rude and insulting to both the officers and the men of the black units.

Almost at once, companies C and D of the 54th were called upon to carry out a combat mission. They were ordered to make a raid on Darien, a village on the coast of Georgia. A small Rebel force was thought to be camped there. Companies C and D were under the command of Lieutenant James

Grace and Captain Ed Jones. But, Colonel Shaw decided to go along. So did General Montgomery, who wanted to see the 54th in action. The Companies left their camp on St. Simon's Island.

All the way to Darien the general made ugly remarks. Right in front of Shaw he insulted the troops saying, "This pack isn't worth the powder it would take to blow them to hell."

On approaching Darien, the men advanced cautiously in skirmish formation. Before them were some white-washed frame houses with neat gardens, a church, a post office, and a general store. As the troops approached, they met no resistance. A house-to-house search turned up nothing. The village was deserted. The people had fled to the mainland, leaving their belongings behind. There was no sign of Confederate troops.

General Montgomery was furious. This was nothing but a wild goose chase. "Burn the village down!" he commanded Shaw.

The colonel was shocked. Why should the villagers lose their homes? And their church? They were civilians. The U.S. Army was not making war on civilians. It was fighting the Confederate Army.

What was more, Shaw felt it was wrong for *black* troops to burn Darien. "Sir, we must not give the enemy a chance to speak against these soldiers," he said quietly to General Montgomery.

The colonel's protest made General Montgomery

even angrier. He answered Shaw with a string of curses and ordered him to reduce Darien to a pile of ashes.

Shaw decided that he had no choice. Montgomery was his commander. To disobey an order from him would mean serious trouble. Reluctantly he carried out the general's orders. He ordered his men to burn Darien.

When he returned to camp, Colonel Shaw wrote to General Hunter, Commanding Officer for the Department of the South. In his letter Shaw told Hunter that Montgomery had ordered him to burn Darien. He also told how the general mistreated the men.

Hunter's reply was short and cutting. Colonel Shaw was to obey the orders of his superior officer *without question*. Hunter had a high regard for General Montgomery and knew him to be a staunch Union man. Montgomery was a man given to harsh discipline. And Shaw was not to expect his troops to receive special treatment.

It was fortunate that the regiment was soon transferred, together with the 1st and 2nd Carolina. The whole brigade became part of General Alfred Terry's division. And the new brigade commander was young General George Strong, an anti-slavery abolitionist, like Colonel Shaw. Almost with a sigh of relief from the whole regiment, the 54th moved from St. Simon's Island to St. Helena, an island close to South Carolina.

11 "Short" Pay

TUESDAY, June 30, was payday.

Till now, the regiment had been paid by the state of Massachusetts. Now for the first time the men of the 54th were going to receive their wages from the federal government. There was excitement in the air, when the bugler blew "Pay Call." The men lined up for their money.

The paymaster sat with the paysheet before him, ready to check off each man's name as he received his month's wages. What was the dismay of the black soldiers when the first man to step up learned that he was down on the paysheet for only $10! And so were they all! Before this, each one had received the full $13 a month which was a soldier's pay.

"What is the meaning of this?" Colonel Shaw demanded of the paymaster when the men appealed to him. "Why are my men getting 'short' pay?"

The paymaster hemmed and hawed. That was the pay. That was the sum on his sheet. He had nothing to do with the amount. The War Department had decided that troops of "African descent" were to be paid $10 a month, not $13. Then too, three out of the ten dollars was being deducted from their wages for "clothing." So black soldiers were really getting only $7.

The colonel was outraged. White soldiers got $13 a month. Why should black soldiers get less?

He was not responsible, said the paymaster. He was only carrying out his orders.

Colonel Shaw explained the situation to the men. He told them what their rights were. There was no reason why they should get less pay than white soldiers. "You are risking your lives the same as any white man," he said, "and should get equal pay for taking that risk."

The regiment took a vote. They all agreed. Every black soldier voted to refuse to accept "short pay." The government was not acting in "good faith." When they enlisted, they had been told that the pay was $13 a month, and it included state aid for families.

At the same time, they told the colonel, they wanted the government in Washington to know that they had not enlisted for the sake of the money.

"We enlisted to destroy slave power," they said. "We will continue to serve loyally *without pay* until the government pays us the same as white soldiers."

Colonel Shaw was proud of the regiment's stand. The federal government was asking black men to risk their lives. But it was also acting as if a black man's life was worth less than a white man's life.

The colonel lost no time in letting Governor Andrew know about the "short" pay. The governor too was outraged. The Massachusetts lawmakers voted to make up the difference. But the regiment would not accept this offer. The 54th flatly refused to take the state's money. The regiment wanted the federal government to keep its word. The men wanted justice as well as pay.

The officers backed up the men. From the colonel to the second lieutenants, every officer in the regiment refused to accept any salary until the troops got their proper pay.

It was an unheard of thing in the army—soldiers and officers standing together. And the fact that the soldiers were black while the officers were white made it even more surprising.

Because of this, people heard what was happening, even in the midst of war. Black and white abolitionists alike began to pressure Congress for an equal pay bill.

Frederick Douglass protested to President Lincoln. Black men should be glad to be soldiers, the President said. In time they will be paid the same as whites. Right now we can't do it. It would make white people too angry.

Meantime, the soldiers themselves were getting angry. This was a strike, And, as in every strike, the ones who suffer most are the families of the strikers. It was this suffering that made the men lose patience. Their families depended on the soldiers' pay. An officer in the 54th wrote: "There is a Sergeant Swails, a man who has fairly won promotion on the field of battle. While he was doing the work of the government in the field, his family and children were placed in the poorhouse."

The 54th was not the only unit getting short pay. By this time there were many black regiments. And all black units were serving as "cheap soldiers." A man in the 8th U.S. Colored Troops wrote, "My wife and three children at home are, in a manner, freezing and starving to death. She writes to me for aid, but I have nothing to send her . . . to answer her letters I must go to some of our officers to get paper and envelopes."

Colonel Higginson of Massachusetts was the white commander of the 1st South Carolina Volunteers—the first black regiment mustered into the Union Army. He protested vigorously to the War Department, but he got nowhere. He wrote desperate letters to anyone who might be able to put pressure on the President and the Congress. To the editor of the New York *Tribune* he wrote: "No one can possibly be so weary of reading of the wrongs done by

Thomas W. Higginson, 1823-1911
Commander of the First South Carolina Volunteers

the government toward the colored soldiers as I am of writing about them."

He warned that there would be violence if the mistake of "short pay" were not corrected. There was some violence. Black soldiers rapidly lost faith in the U.S. government. Many refused to fight for a country that had betrayed them.

Sergeant William Walker of the 3rd South Carolina Volunteers was one man who refused to fight. Walker marched his company to his captain's tent and ordered the men to stack arms and resign from an army that broke its contract with them. Sergeant Walker was court-martialed, then shot for mutiny.

Higginson complained bitterly that the U.S. government was forcing officers of the South Carolina regiments "to act as executioners for those soldiers who, like Sergeant Walker, refused to fulfill their share of a contract where the government has openly repudiated the other share."

Not until June 15, 1864, did Congress correct the injustice of short pay. The men got their full $13 a month. They also got equal back pay for the 18 months they had served without salary. James Ruffin, a sergeant in the 55th Massachusetts wrote to his sister-in-law after the paymaster had visited the regiment: "We had a glorious celebration, there was a procession, then a mass meeting where speeches . . . were made. . . . In the evening we had a Grand Supper."

The point had been made. A black man's life was worth the same as a white man's. It was hard for all men to die. But all men died equal.

12 We're Off to See the Elephant

EVEN BEFORE their second payless payday rolled
around, the 54th was to "see the elephant." The
regiment had been on St. Helena about three weeks
when their marching orders came: Proceed to Folly
Island at the mouth of the Stone River.

The trip was no joy ride. The crowded transports
were only slightly better than cattle boats, and the
quarters for the officers and men were unbelievably
bad. Fortunately the trip was short. By daybreak,
July 9, the transports were at anchor off Folly
Island, just a few miles south of Charleston.

All around them the men saw other vessels—

transports loaded with troops, supply ships, men-of-war, and gunboats. They were seeing one of the most powerful naval squadrons brought together during the Civil War. Aboard the transports alone there were 10,000 infantrymen, 350 artillerymen, and 600 engineers.

Why had this mighty force gathered here? There was to be a grand attack on the outer defenses of Charleston. Those defenses were Fort Sumter, James Island, and Morris Island. And at the northern tip of Morris Island stood the greatest stronghold of all—Fort Wagner. More than any of the other forts, Fort Wagner prevented the Union Army from capturing Charleston. If Fort Wagner fell, it would be very difficult for the Rebels to hold Charleston—the city that was capital of the first state to leave the Union; the city that was the seat of rebellion and disunion.

Admiral John Dahlgren was in command of the massive naval squadron anchored off Folly Island. He was confident he could take Fort Wagner, the massive Morris Island battery. His plan was well thought-out, it was down on paper, and he was certain it would work.

First of all, strong points on James Island had to be battered down. Then Fort Sumter must be knocked out. In addition the shore batteries all around Charleston Harbor must be silenced. When all this had been done, an attack could be made on Fort Wagner itself. Union guns would pound

the fort to rubble. Then the infantry would storm it. It was all down on paper.

Union troops were already landed on Morris Island. Their job was to secure the approach to Fort Wagner. But heavy fire from Confederates located at James Island, Fort Sumter, and the shore batteries had these Union troops pinned down on their beachhead. If they remained trapped, they would be unable to prepare the way for the attack on Fort Wagner.

On July 11, the 54th was ordered to James Island. A blazing sun beat down and not a breath of air was stirring. Still, the sweating soldiers joyfully climbed down the landing nets to the boats below. After two days and three nights on their transports, the men were happy to have solid ground under their feet again.

The 54th had no sooner landed on the beach than Brigadier General Stevenson called Shaw and his staff to a conference. The general wanted the 54th to go immediately into action on James Island. There a furious battle was underway. Three white regiments were attacking the Confederates. But the Rebels, trying to keep the Union forces from capturing the island, were striking back hard. Still, the Confederates had a weakness. They were trying to do two jobs at once so their forces were spread thin.

John A. Dahlgren, 1809-1870

They had to defend their own positions on James Island while trying to help keep the Union forces on Morris Island pinned down on their beachhead.

General Stevenson's plan was to force the Confederates to fight on one front only. He had to make them use the guns now bombarding Morris Island to defend their own positions on James Island. To do this he needed three companies from the 54th to help his men at the front. These combined companies would make an all-out attack on the James Island positions and force the Rebels to fight for their lives.

General Stevenson gave Shaw one hour to get his men ready.

Shaw hurried back to his men at the beach. The word passed quickly: "We're going to see the elephant."

When "Assembly Call" sounded, the men raced to their places in line. Companies D, E, and F were ordered to move at once to the battlefront with Colonel Shaw. The rest of the regiment, commanded by Edward Hallowell, were to follow closely but to wait for further orders.

For the time being, they all waited.

In less than an hour the 54th had drawn its ammunition and was in marching order. Now, the men stood leaning on their rifles waiting for word from brigade headquarters to move out. Even the liveliest, most talkative fellows seemed to be lost in thought. The sounds of rifle and cannon fire reminded them that the moment for which they had been so long preparing was almost at hand. Soon they would be getting their first real taste of war.

Shaw studied the serious faces of the men. Through the months together, those faces had grown familiar. How would the men fight? Which of them would be brave? Who would prove to be a coward? Who among them would be dead or maimed before the sun went down? And what of himself, their commander? No man could tell beforehand how he would react under fire. Would he be the one to flee the battlefield? Silently, he vowed not to fail his men.

At 3:30 P.M., a rider galloped up to Colonel Shaw. He saluted and cried out: "The general wants you to move at once! March to the sound of the guns!"

13 "I Can Promise You, Gentlemen..."

By 4:15 P.M., Companies D, E, and F of the 54th were in battle. They were "seeing the elephant" at last. And just as those first black troops had fought gallantly under fire, so did the men of the 54th. They met their test and stood their ground. When an enemy attack drove back the 10th Connecticut Volunteers, the blacks covered the retreat of the white soldiers and smashed the Rebel charge.

That night, under cover of darkness, the Rebels left James Island. The Union troops stayed on the alert all night. At daybreak, companies D, E, and F were relieved of front line duty.

The weary men stumbled back into camp. On the way they had to pass the camp of the 10th Connecticut. The whites burst into applause as the battle-stained blacks marched by, and the colonel of the white regiment said to Shaw: "Your troops saved mine. Tell your splendid black soldiers that we are proud to call them comrades!"

After that day's fighting, there was little for the 54th to do on James Island except stand guard and wait for what would come next. The rumor that there would be an all-out attack on Fort Wagner kept everybody on edge. They all knew that the troops which had been landed on Morris Island were now holding the beachhead. And every day the 54th heard the big navy guns pounding away at Fort Sumter. The men suspected that a big battle was in the making.

On July 16, Colonel Shaw received word that on the 17th the 54th was to move to Morris Island. That evening Colonel Shaw told the troops about the order he had received. "Men," he said, "we shall soon be in an important battle on Morris Island. The eyes of the nation will be upon us. I know you will not let the country down!"

Sergeant Lewis Douglass, eldest son of Frederick Douglass, wrote his father that night: "By the time you get this letter, I will have been in battle. If I do not survive, know this, I am not afraid to die if my death will mean freedom for our people. See to it, Father. See to it that our sacrifice will not have been made in vain . . . ."

The next afternoon, the 54th boarded a transport and moved to Folly Island. The regiment then marched across the island to another transport.

And just as darkness was falling, they were put ashore on Morris Island. At the opposite end of the island stood massive Fort Wagner. It was not more than 1,000 yards away.

The regiment had hardly settled down for the night when Colonel Shaw was called to a meeting at the headquarters of General Gillmore. Gillmore was in charge of all the land operations. He had summoned the commanders of regiments and brigades to hear some important news. On the evening of the following day, an attack would be made on Fort Wagner.

The fort was immense. For 630 feet it stretched across the whole northern tip of the island. Built of sand and turf, it had a facing of sturdy palmetto logs. On its east side lay the Atlantic Ocean. A creek and bottomless marshes were on the west. Thus the fort could be approached only from the south. But on the south, Fort Wagner was protected by guns of every size. And less than two miles away were the guns of Fort Sumter as well as the many shore batteries. All these guns guarded the approach to Fort Wagner.

As if this were not enough, the fort had thick parapets that provided excellent cover for Rebel gunners. And deep, bomb-proof dugouts provided shelter for the 1,700 men garrisoned in the fort.

People called Fort Wagner *impregnable*—impossible to take. But General Gillmore was convinced that it could and would be taken. The

The Charleston fleet of ironclads.

A battery—a fortlike structure
with many gunports.

fortress would be reduced to rubble, he said. The naval squadron of Admiral Dahlgren would do that. At daybreak his ships would start battering Fort Wagner, Fort Sumter, and all the shore batteries. This naval bombardment would continue on until after sundown. Then the troops would attack.

"I can promise you, gentlemen," the general said, "that there will be almost no one left alive in Fort Wagner when our guns have finished with the place." If any of the garrison should be left, the general said, they would be so dazed by the explosions that they would not be able to resist.

Admiral Dahlgren of the U.S. Navy was present at the meeting. He picked up where General Gillmore left off. The admiral was forceful. "Not only will we silence the guns and crush the garrison," he said, "but we will also batter down the parapets." Under his bombardment, he said, Fort Wagner would crumble.

Shaw left the meeting feeling very hopeful. He told the officers of his regiment that the next day would bring "glory to the 54th."

Shaw's confidence was shared by his men. They sat around the campfires singing and talking. The next day's battle was hardly mentioned.

There was just one hint that the soldiers were worried. They kept cleaning their weapons. They looked over every cartridge. They oiled their rifles, rammed the barrels, and checked the mechanisms again and again.

94

14 "We'll Be Honored"

THE 54TH awoke to the sound of cannons—and remembered. This was the day.

The sun had not yet risen. Only its first pale rays lit up the eastern sky. In the pre-dawn light, the soldiers could just make out the shadowy bulk of the warships riding at their battle stations. The air was fresh. Waves rolled shoreward in an endless line and broke upon the beach. Spray leaped up. Foam caught the sun's first beams. On this lovely morning the warships seemed out of place. It was a day for living, not for killing or dying.

Saturday, July 18, 1863. This day Fort Wagner was to fall. Colonel Shaw recalled the confident face of General Gillmore the night before. He remembered the forceful words: "I can promise you . . .

there will be almost no one left alive . . . when our guns have finished with the place."

Now the colonel looked toward the fort. Black smoke from exploding shells ringed it like a huge wreath. Bright stabs of red flame cut the smoke as the missiles struck.

It would be a long day before evening came and the troops were called upon to play their part. The daylight hours belonged to the navy. General Gillmore said this would be the greatest naval bombardment in history. It was indeed something to see.

"What a serenade the guns gave us," a soldier later recalled. Squinting their eyes against the sun, the troops watched the firing. Sometimes they looked toward Fort Wagner. Sometimes they shifted their gaze to Fort Sumter, which was also veiled in gunsmoke. They looked to the distant fires along the shoreline—fires which showed where cannons had scored direct hits on the shore batteries.

Very quickly the air that had been so fresh when the camp awoke became filled with gunsmoke. Men coughed and choked on it. It filled everybody's nostrils. It rolled in a black stream from the muzzles of the cannons and, rising, partly hid the sun. From hour to hour the bombardment grew more furious.

Moving in a long single column, the ships sailed back and forth, firing broadside after broadside. The earth shook with the blasts of the thundering guns. A soldier remembered, "The noise was like a huge bass drum which some mad giant was pounding."

THE ATTACK ON FORT WAGNER
Charleston Harbor and Surrounding Fortifications

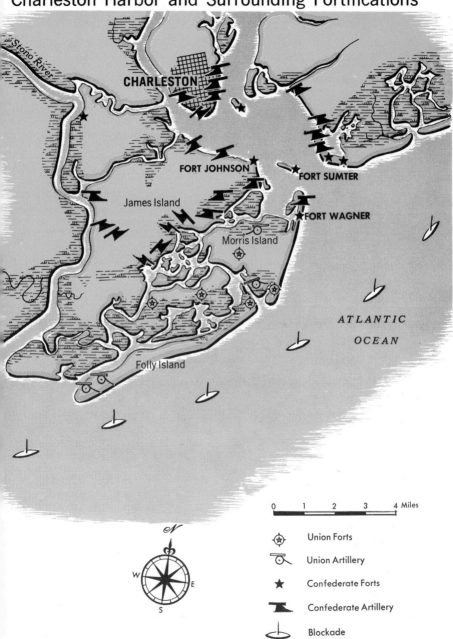

CHARLESTON

Stono River

FORT JOHNSON

FORT SUMTER

FORT WAGNER

James Island

Morris Island

ATLANTIC OCEAN

Folly Island

0   1   2   3   4 Miles

N
W   E
S

⊛ Union Forts

🔫 Union Artillery

★ Confederate Forts

◣ Confederate Artillery

⊥ Blockade

The Union soldiers knew that 1,700 men were inside Fort Wagner. A black soldier said solemnly, "I feel sorry for Johnny Reb. That place must be hell on earth."

Listening to the guns, many felt sorry for "Johnny Reb." The firing was almost continuous. Several times the supply ships had to send more ammunition to the battleships and gunboats. But as the day wore on, the gunners could not keep up so rapid a rate of firing. The heat in the gun turrets was almost unbearable, and the men had to rest. The shots began to come less often. Though less furious, the bombardment was still fierce.

At about four o'clock in the afternoon, a group of officers rode up to Colonel Shaw's tent. General Strong, brigade commander, dismounted. Tall, trim, broad-shouldered, with a saber and sword at his waist, he stood towering over Shaw.

"We're going to storm Fort Wagner at twilight," the general said. "Would you like your regiment to be the shock troop?"

"We'll be honored!" Shaw replied without hesitation.

Strong nodded. "The post is yours." The general swung back on to his horse. Shaw saluted, and Strong cantered off, followed by his staff officers.

Shaw's face was stern, but his heart was pounding with excitement. He turned to Hallowell, "Form the regiment. I want to tell the men."

When the troops assembled, Shaw gave them the

news: the 54th was to lead the attack on Fort Wagner! It was hard to tell just what effect the news had on the men, but there was a difference. Of all the troops on Morris Island they would serve in the very forefront of battle.

Late in the afternoon, Shaw was told the order of battle. The 54th was to storm the right flank of the fort, the side nearest the ocean. The 24th Massachusetts, the 10th Connecticut, and the 97th Pennsylvania would move in behind the 54th.

The right flank and the center would be stormed by the 52nd and the 104th Pennsylvania and the 56th New York. General Strong himself would lead the right flank. The U.S. Colored Troops—the 1st and 2nd Carolinas—would act as their support.

The attack was to begin at 7:45 P.M., five minutes after the bombardment stopped. The signal to move out would be three red rockets sent up by the *New Ironsides*. At brigade headquarters, a signal gun would also be fired.

The 54th was to attack three companies abreast, in triple ranks. Company K would be the color company. It would carry the flag and lead the shock troops.

The guns of the Union Navy still thundered. Admiral Dahlgren had no way of telling what damage the pounding of his guns was doing, but he felt he knew. There could be but one result— Fort Wagner must crumble.

There was none to tell the admiral that he was mistaken. He did not know that the terrible day-long shelling was causing far less damage than he expected. The shells did not blast down the parapets as he thought. Instead, the soft sand absorbed much of the shock.

When the guns of Fort Wagner did not fire back at his ships, Admiral Dahlgren was overjoyed. "I've silenced the enemy batteries," he said. But he was mistaken. Most of the guns were still safe and sound.

The fort's big guns he had counted on destroying had hardly been touched. For, as soon as the bombardment started, the gunners had hauled the pieces back and covered them with sandbags. Thus the only guns destroyed or damaged were the few that were hit in the first moments of the bombardment.

There were very few casualties among the Confederate soldiers in the fort. Some men had been caught in the open when the shooting started. But most of the men weathered the bombardment in dugouts and trenches.

Of all this the Union soldiers and their commanders were unaware. They thought they were preparing to storm a fort that had crumbled. They were certain the men inside the fort were too dazed from the explosions to resist.

The soldiers guarding the Union Army camp on Morris Island had to check the pass of each person entering and leaving the area.

"Moving in a long single column, the ships sailed back and forth, firing broadside after broadside."

"The blacks fell in heaps, cut down by the rain of bullets. For a few seconds their comrades stood still,

confused. They heard the wounded screaming. They
saw the dead lying sprawled where they had fallen."

"Every second man carried a stretcher."

They planted the flags on the parapet, then fought furiously to defend them.

"Wherever they fought, black troops brought honor to themselves and the Union cause."

First South Carolina Volunteers attacked by Confederate dogs trained for war.

Assault of the Second Louisiana Regiment on the
Confederate works at Port Hudson.

In the Battle of Milliken's Bend 1,000 untrained black
soldiers defeated a force of 2,000 Confederates.

Martin R. Delany, 104th Regiment at Charleston. First
black officer to gain the rank of Major.

15 "Forward, 54th! Forward!"

At 5:30 p.m., General Strong sent word that he was coming to inspect the 54th in half an hour. He wanted the regiment in marching order, ready to move out.

At 5:45, "Assembly" was sounded, and the troops fell in.

"Fix bayonets!" Shaw commanded.

There was a clatter of metal. Then a silence broken only by the continuing naval bombardment.

Exactly at 6 o'clock, General Strong and his staff galloped into the camp. The handsome abolitionist general rode along the regimental line and nodded his satisfaction. The ranks were perfectly in line, the soldiers at attention, their eyes straight ahead, the points of their bayonets glittering. At the head of the troops were the colors. The officers stood with swords drawn in salute. Everything was very correct.

General Strong raised himself in his stirrups, whipped off his hat, and pointed toward Fort Wagner.

"Men!" he cried in a ringing voice. "Black men! You soon will come to grips with the slavemasters! Black free men! In your courage and strength lies the hope of your persecuted people! Strike off the shackles of slavery that bind them! Wipe out the shame the slavers have inflicted on your long-suffering race!

"Black men! You will take that damned fort! I know you will do it! And don't forget that we, whose skin is white, will be with you, sharing your perils and dangers! Do not flinch!

"Will you follow the flag to victory?"

A great shout went up from the ranks. "Yes! Yes!"

Turning to the man carrying the Stars and Stripes, Strong said: "Who will take this flag if the bearer should fall?"

Sergeant Will Carney called out: "I'll take it, sir! That old flag'll never touch the ground if I can help it!"

"That's the spirit!" the general said. And with a wave of his hat, he wheeled his horse and galloped off, shouting, "Victory! Victory!"

When General Strong had gone, Shaw ordered the men to rest until time to move out. Then he spoke with Hallowell.

"I shall go in advance with the national flag,"

Shaw said. "You keep the state flag and the regimental colors with you. It will give the men something to rally around. Good luck! We shall take that fort or die!"

The two men shook hands. Hallowell took his place at the left of the line, Shaw to the right. The sun had set, and the light had begun to fade. It was nearly time to move forward. The troops got to their feet.

Suddenly they all became aware of something strange. It was the silence. The guns had stopped booming. Now, the swish of the surf and the cry of night birds could be heard.

Colonel Shaw walked over to the color bearer with the national flag. A lighted cigar in his hand, he addressed the 54th for the last time before the attack.

"Men!" he said. "You must prove yourselves tonight. You are a model for the black people. Be brave! Be proud! Follow the colors! Good luck, and may God bless you all!"

Three red-tailed rockets hissed up from the *New Ironsides*. At the same time the signal gun went off with one sound of a heavy door being slammed. It was exactly 7:45 P.M.

"Move in quick time until within 100 yards of the fort" Shaw commanded. "Then double quick and charge! Go in and bayonet them at their guns!" Whipping out his sword, he raised it high. "Forward, 54th! Forward!" he shouted.

111

16 "In Sorrow and Grief — But Not in Shame"

WITH CIGAR clenched between his teeth, Shaw strode ahead. Behind him came the regiment. Night was closing in fast, and the first stars appeared in the sky. But not one man looked up to see them. Every eye was on Fort Wagner.

Suddenly, shells from a Confederate shore battery slammed into the earth near the color company. The enemy had made out the flags moving along the beach. The color bearers saw that the flags were giving the enemy a target and began to furl them. But Captain Simpkins called out: "Unfurl those colors! The Rebs know we're here. Let 'em see us with our colors flying!"

At this the bearers raised their standards again, and the lines pushed on as though on parade. In the rear marched the regimental band. Instead of instruments, every second man carried a stretcher. It was the band's duty to act as stretcher-bearers.

As the regiment advanced, the beach on the right grew narrower. In order to keep the ranks unbroken, the men on the right went knee deep into the ocean. On the left, marsh grass tore at uniforms. Men stumbled over roots. But though the lines were no longer perfect, the 54th struggled on.

Shells from distant Confederate shore batteries continued now and then to dig up the earth in front and behind them. From Fort Wagner itself there wasn't a shot. Like a monster, the fortress loomed in the settling dark. Smoke still swirled over the parapets. But there was no sound, no sign of life, nothing to show that the garrison was still alive after the naval pounding and that hundreds of riflemen crouched silently on the walls.

When the front line of the 54th was some 300 yards from the outerworks of the fort, the moon suddenly came out from behind a cloud. Now the attacking Union forces could be plainly seen. Rebel gunners on the opposite shore fired shell after shell at them until the *New Ironsides* moved up to blast the batteries.

Suddenly, at 200 yards, the 54th heard a shout from a parapet: "Open fire!"

A sheet of flame leaped along the wall as

hundreds of Rebels fired from Fort Wagner. The blacks fell in heaps, cut down by the rain of bullets. For a few seconds their comrades stood still, confused. They heard the wounded screaming. They saw the dead lying sprawled where they had fallen. But before the enemy had time to fire a second volley, Shaw sprang into action. Waving his sword overhead, he shouted: "Charge! At the double! Charge!"

Hearing his voice, the regiment recovered. The colors moved ahead. The 54th rushed toward the fort, bayonets leveled. Every man was yelling fiercely as he had been trained to do when charging with a bayonet. Another volley raked the blacks. More men fell. But the advance did not stop. The men ran on, bent double, as though pressing into a rainstorm.

From the fort, the enemy met the oncoming men with shrapnel, fired from cannon. The blacks crumpled. Dead and horribly wounded, they fell as they ran forward. Somehow a few stayed alive. The color bearers swarmed up to the top of a parapet.

They planted the state and regimental flags on the parapet, then fought furiously to defend them. In the hand-to-hand fighting, Edward Hallowell dropped, wounded in the stomach. A husky private lifted him up and carried him back to a shell hole.

Meantime, the rest of Hallowell's men had also reached the parapet. But they were forced back with heavy losses. Before retreating, however, the bearers rescued their colors. On the right of the line, Shaw clambered to the top of the parapet with the flag bearer a step behind him.

The color guard fell, wounded. Even as he fell, Sergeant Carney, true to his word, caught the flag before it touched the ground.

Shaw moved his men on, yelling: "Rally, 54th! Rally!" Suddenly he pitched forward off the wall into the fort. He had been shot through the heart.

The wild fray lasted no more than ten minutes before the Rebels drove off the Union soldiers. The retreating men took cover in shell holes. From there they kept shooting at the parapet to prevent the Rebels from coming out to counterattack. Meanwhile, the fort's guns blasted the brigade coming up to support the 54th. Only a handful of these support troops managed to reach what remained of the 54th.

On other parts of the line it was the same. The men were cut down by deadly Confederate fire. General Strong led a desperate charge. He was shot through the head and was carried off by his men to die.

The storming of Fort Wagner was a military disaster. Of the 22 officers who had gone into the action, three were dead. Eleven others were wounded. Captain Luis Emilio was the highest ranking officer left, and the men regrouped under him.

When the captain led the survivors back into camp, only about half the fighting 54th regiment was left. Of the 660 who had taken part in the attack, 117 had been killed, 149 wounded, and 52 were missing. The men were dazed, weary, heartsick. They wept for their fallen comrades. Some of these lay stretched on the ocean beach, dead, dying, wounded. Others still lay in the sand holes and rifle pits where they had crept to die. There was but one consolation for the 54th—they had fought gallantly.

"You and your missing comrades have spilled your blood," Captain Emilio told them next morning. "We were defeated, and we may bow our heads in sorrow and grief—but not in shame."

General Gillmore sent some officers under a white flag to ask the Rebels for Colonel Shaw's body. The Rebel general refused. "We've buried him with his niggers where he belongs!" he told the Union officers.

It was a remark not soon forgotten. Black men flocked to enlist in the 54th regiment.

Before the war ended, more than 180,000 black men bore arms. Most served as infantry, but there were black artillery, cavalry, and engineer units too. These troops fought in more than a hundred battles, skirmishes, and actions.

Wherever they fought, black troops brought honor to themselves and the Union cause. Sixteen black soldiers and four black sailors were awarded the

Sergeant W. H. Carney, flagbearer for the 54th.
He won the Congressional Medal of Honor for
his bravery under fire.

Congressional Medal of Honor.

In all, about 38,000 black soldiers gave their lives in defense of the Union and to put an end to slavery.

But what of those men of the 54th who lived to return home? And what of the freedom of black people for which they had fought?

"See to it, father," the eldest son of Frederick Douglas had written on the eve of battle, "See to it that our sacrifices will not have been made in vain."

In the years right after the Civil War, it did not seem that brave black men had died in vain. Rather, this was a time of great hope.

For in these years, the law of the land—the United States Constitution—was changed to give black Americans the same freedom it gave to white Americans.

In 1865, the Thirteenth Amendment did away with slavery.

Amendment 13

Section 1. Neither slavery nor involuntary servitude, except as a punishment for crime whereof the party shall have been duly convicted, shall exist within the United States, or any place subject to their jurisdiction.

Section 2. Congress shall have power to enforce this article by appropriate legislation.

In 1868, the Fourteenth Amendment said that *all* persons born in the United States were citizens and that *no* state could take away the rights given to citizens by the Constitution.

Amendment 14

Section 1. All persons born or naturalized in the United States, and subject to the jurisdiction thereof, are citizens of the United States and of the State wherein they reside. No State shall make or enforce any law which shall abridge the privileges or immunities of citizens of the United States; nor shall any State deprive any person of life, liberty, or property, without due process of law; nor deny to any person within its jurisdiction the equal protection of the laws.

In 1870, the Fifteenth Amendment said that no citizen could have his rights taken away because of race or color or because he had once been a slave.

Amendment 15

Section 1. The right of citizens of the United States to vote shall not be denied or abridged by the United States or by any State on account of race, color, or previous condition of servitude.

Section 2. The Congress shall have power to enforce this article by appropriate legislation.

The law of the land said plainly that black citizens too could vote and run for office, that they could go to school, work, and live a full life as did white citizens.

When the black soldiers laid down their guns and went home, they tasted some of these freedoms. But not for long.

The southern Rebels who had lost on the battlefield won back their power over the lives of black Americans. They did this with beatings, murder, trickery, and state laws that openly defied the U.S. Constitution.

Ten years after the Civil War, the battle for true freedom for black Americans had been lost. It was a battle that would have to be fought again.

But, as Frederick Douglass vowed long ago, "Somewhere yonder lies the gold of freedom. The way to the treasure is hard, the road long. . . . But *we shall persevere, we shall endure, we shall overcome some day!*"

Index

(Page numbers of illustrations are in bold type.)

rigid health rules, 51
as shock troop, 98
training of, 50, 60
transferred, 77
trouble at Camp Meigs, 47
trouble with Gen.
  Montgomery, 75-77
waiting for battle, 91
Fort Wagner
battle of, 92-94, 99-100,
  112-116
greatest Confederate
  stronghold, 85
Fourteenth Amendment, 119

G

Garnet, Henry Highland, 30,
  30
Garrison, William Lloyd, 56
Gillmore, Gen., 92, 95, 116
Grace, Lt. James W., 34,
  75-76
Grant, President Ulysses, 11

H

Haggerty, Annie, 25-26, 38
becomes Mrs. Shaw, 62
Hallowell, Lt. Col. Edward,
  68, 88, 110-111
dies in battle, 114
Hallowell, Col. Norwood, 25
to command second black
  regiment, 54

inspects training camp,
  35-36
Higginson, Col. Thomas,
  81-82, **82**
Hunter, Gen. David, **58**, 59, 77

J

Jones, Capt. Ed, 75-76

L

Langston, Charles, 30
Langston, John, 30, **30**
Lee, Gen. Robert E., 11, 18
Lincoln, President Abraham,
  10-11
and border-state slaves, 20
Emancipation
  Proclamation of, 18
hated by Copperheads,
  32-33
no black soldiers, 12
"short" pay, 80-81
turns down Governor
  Andrew, 17

M

Manassas, 9, 18
medical rules, 34, 51
Montgomery, Gen. James, 68
"Burn the village down,"
  76-77
trouble with 54th, 75

Thirteenth Amendment, 118
Turner, Henry M., 30

U

Union Army, 10
Union
   Europe supports, 21
   slavery ends, 18
Unionists, 12

U.S. Colored Troops, 68, 81;
   see also Corps d'Afrique

V

volunteers, 10

W

Walker, Sgt. William, 82-83
Wall, O. S. B., 30

Photo Acknowledgments

Culver Pictures, Inc.: pp. 19, 24, 39-40 *(bottom)*, 101-103, 104 *(top)*; Milton Meltzer: pp. 30-31, 33, 39 *(top)*, 41 *(top)*, 42-43, 44 *(bottom)*, 45-46, 69-72, 74, 82, 105-108, 117; Library of Congress: pp. 41 *(bottom)*, 44 *(top)*, 58, 86; Negro History Associates: pp. 8, 55, 73, 93; New York Historical Society: p. 17; New York Public Library, Rare Book Division: p. 40 *(top)*; New York Public Library, Schonburg Collection: p. 104 *(bottom)*; Photoworld, Inc.: p. 11; Virginia State Library: p. 11